RAIN

Franklin Watts Limited
26 Albemarle Street
London W1

Thanks are due to the following for kind
permission to reproduce photographs:

Anglo-Chilean Society; BBC Photograph
Library; Negretti and Zambra Limited;
Oxfam; Radio Times Hulton Picture Library;
Philip Sauvain; Swiss National Tourist Office;
Syndication International; Thames Water
Authority; Welsh National Water Development
Authority.

Cover illustration by courtesy of Cameric
Photographic Library/E. H. Lumb.

Printed in Great Britain by
BAS Printers Limited, Over Wallop, Hampshire

RAIN

by
Philip Sauvain

Illustrated by
Elizabeth Haines

FRANKLIN WATTS
London and New York

Imagine what would happen if more **rain** fell
on your home town in one day than usually
falls in a month.

Occasionally, this does happen when the
rainfall is extremely heavy.

Having too much rain, which can cause
flooding, is disastrous.

But having too little rain can also be a disaster.

The ground dries up so that nothing can grow,
and there is a shortage of water.

When there is no rain for a long period, it is
called a **drought.**

In most places people can be sure that there
will be some rain during the year, although
there are some places in the world where dry
weather lasts for years.
In the **Atacama Desert** in Chile, there are
places which have had no rain for over four
hundred years.

The Sahara desert. Camels are often used for desert transport

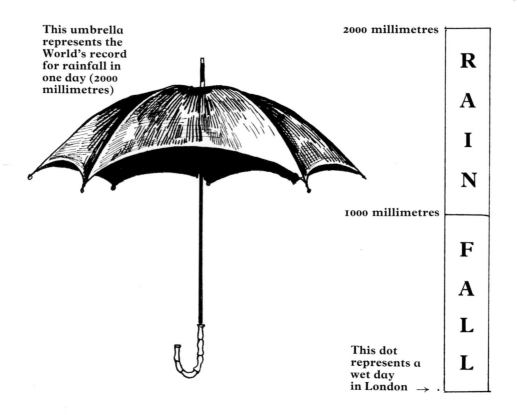

This umbrella represents the World's record for rainfall in one day (2000 millimetres)

2000 millimetres

R
A
I
N

1000 millimetres

F
A
L
L

This dot represents a wet day in London → .

It is a good thing, too, not to get heavy rain very often.

One island in the Indian Ocean once got enough rain in one day to cover the land with water over two metres (6 feet) deep!

This was about one thousand times as much rain as that which usually falls on London on a wet day.

When a lot of rain falls in a short time, the
   rivers fill up with **water.**
If it keeps on raining, the sides of the river
   (river **banks**) are like the sides of a bath
   when the tap is left running.
The water spills over the banks of the river and
   floods over the fields or houses.

People being rescued from flooded houses

Clearing away mud and rubbish left by floods

Flooding can do a lot of damage.

Houses and villages have been washed away by
streams bursting their banks, and sometimes
people are drowned.

One of the worst floods ever recorded happened
in China in 1931, when four million people
were drowned when the Hwang-ho river
flooded.

Although heavy rain does a lot of damage, we
could not live without rain.
Therefore, rainfall is very important in our
lives.
If there was no water to **drink,** we would die.
Plants and **animals** need water, too.
In hot, dry countries very few plants can grow,
or animals live, if left without water.

The remains of animals unable to survive without water

Modern irrigation—nozzles on the pipes whirl round and round, spraying water over a large area

In summer you may be glad when day after
   day the weather is hot and dry.
But while you sunbathe, **farmers** will be
   looking at their fields, worried that their
   crops will not grow well without rain.
Sometimes they water their plants from pipes
   laid out in rows in the fields.
This is called **irrigation.**

Some plants need a lot of water in which to
  grow.
In China, Malaysia and India, **rice** is grown in
  paddy fields in the summer.
"Paddy" is the Malaysian word for rice.
The small rice plants have to be planted in wet
  fields.
The rice farmers hope that heavy rain will
  flood the fields with water.

Planting rice

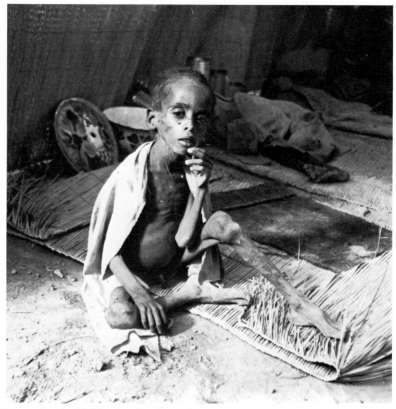

Child starving in Ethiopia. As there has been little or no rain for a number of years, people are unable to grow food

If the rains do not come, the rice harvest is very
    poor and there is a **famine.**
A famine means that there is no food.
This means that thousands of people will not
    get enough food to eat, and they may even
    starve to death.

In most years Britain and Northern Europe get plenty of rain.

People usually grumble that there is too much rain, not too little.

However, in 1976 most places in Britain and Northern Europe had the driest, and warmest, summer for many years.

The water in the ground, and in the **ponds** and **reservoirs** dried up.

This reservoir is normally full of water, but during the summer of 1976 it dried up completely

Umbrella shops did very badly, for no one
wanted to buy an umbrella in the summer of
1976!
Many crops were ruined, and precious flowers
and plants died because people were not able
to water them.

In some places in Britain, the water supply was
cut off for seventeen hours every day.
In others, people had to get their water from
special taps in the streets called **standpipes.**
The British drought of 1976 came to an end in
September when heavy rain fell.
Many parts of the country had much more
than their usual rainfall that autumn.

As you can see, **rainfall** is very important
   indeed.

Scientists have tried to make rain by sending
   aeroplanes into the clouds to sow them with
   rain pellets!

So far these experiments have had some
   success, but there is little hope of bringing
   severe droughts to an end in this way.

We still have to rely on the **weather** and the
   sea.

We rely on the sea because at the start that is where most of our rainfall comes from.

You may find this surprising because you know that sea water is very salty and very unpleasant to taste if you get it in your mouth when swimming.

But sea water **evaporates** and this forms **rain clouds.**

When water turns into a **vapour** it is said to
evaporate.

You will have seen at home that when water
turns to steam, it turns from **liquid** to
vapour.

We do not usually see this vapour in the air,
except when it leaves the spout of a boiling
kettle, or in a steamed-up bathroom.

When a wet bathing costume is hung outside on
a clothes line to dry, the water in it
evaporates into the air.

On a hot day the bathing costume is soon dry
and ready to be worn again.

The water in the costume has become **water
vapour.**

It is there in the air even though we cannot
see it.

On some days the wet costume will take a long
time to dry.

This happens when the weather is colder and
everything feels damp.

There is too much water vapour in the air
then.

If the weather gets warmer, the air can take up
more water vapour.

If the weather gets colder, it cannot hold all the
water vapour so this forms **droplets** (small
drops) of water.

At night (when the weather usually gets colder)
water vapour forms droplets of water on cold
surfaces, such as on the ground or on
window-panes.

This is why grass is wet in the morning in
summer, even though there has been no rain
during the night.

The water on the ground in the morning is
called **dew.**

Not all the water vapour turns into dew.

Most of it turns into **rain.**

If there is dust in the air, the droplets of water
collect around each dust particle.
This forms **fog**.
Fog is made up of billions and billions of tiny
droplets of water hanging in the air.

During the day the water evaporates from the
    sea (and also from lakes and rivers) and rises
    into the air.

The water vapour goes higher and higher and,
    as it **cools,** it forms into tiny droplets of
    water floating in the sky.

They collect together to form clouds.

Many of the droplets stay in the clouds for a
long time.

But, if the clouds get colder, some of the tiny
droplets join up with others to form larger
droplets.

When they become too heavy to float in the
cloud, they fall to the ground – as
raindrops.

Heavy rainstorm

Often the droplets become so cold, they turn
into small **pellets** of **ice,** and these join up
with bigger pellets, which also drop towards
the ground.

As they fall they get warmer, and begin to
melt.

At last they, too, fall to the ground as
raindrops.

But in cold weather they may not melt at all,
and we get **snow.**
Sometimes the ice pellets get bigger as they
fall, and then we get a **hailstorm.**
Hailstones are hard pellets of ice, and can be
as large as a golf ball!

Rain or snow falls when the water vapour in
    the clouds gets colder.
It gets colder when the clouds rise higher in the
    sky.
This sometimes happens in summer on a very
    hot day.
You can see the clouds climbing up into the
    sky.

As they tower above us, we can see that the
    lower parts of these clouds have become
    black.
Suddenly everything goes still and the air is
    heavy (or "close").
People begin to feel hot and sticky and tired.

Then, a jagged flash of **lightning** shoots
   across the sky, followed a few seconds later
   by a loud crash.

A **thunderstorm** is on its way.

You can tell how far a thunderstorm is distant
   if you count the seconds in between each
   flash of lightning and the crash of thunder
   which follows.

The lightning is about one kilometre away for
   every three seconds (one mile for every five

seconds) you count.

So, if there is lightning and a crash of thunder
fifteen seconds later, you know that the centre
of the thunderstorm is about five kilometres
(three miles) away.

Thunder rain is usually very heavy.

It can be exciting to watch a thunderstorm
from inside a house, with the pouring rain on
the street outside, and occasional great
flashes of lightning and cracks of thunder.

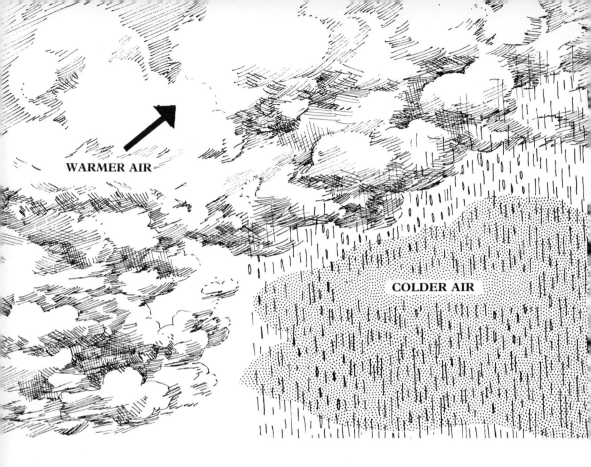

WARMER AIR

COLDER AIR

Much of the rain which falls in Western Europe
is caused when **warm air,** which has come
from warm seas, meets **cold air** which has
come from the polar regions.

The warmer air **rises** over the colder air.

As it rises, it gets cooler and the water vapour
turns into large droplets of water (or into ice
pellets) and these fall as rain.

Rain also falls when the clouds rise in the sky
   in order to climb over **hills.**
Again, they get colder and the water droplets
   turn into rain.
This is why areas with high mountains usually
   get more rainfall than places lower down.

CLOUDS RISING
ABOVE MOUNTAINS

Areas over 1000 feet (305 metres)

Areas with over 40 inches (1015 mm) of rain in a year

In Britain, the English Lake District, the Welsh Mountains and the Scottish Highlands on the **western** side of the country are all much wetter than the flat lowlands of the eastern side.

The western slopes of the Rocky Mountains in North America are wetter than the prairie lands to the east of the mountains.

We know this because at different places the amount of rain which falls each day is **measured.**

It is collected in a special can which is known as a **rain gauge.**

The depth of the rainfall is measured in millimetres.

The people who measure the rainfall have to make sure that the water collected in the gauge does not evaporate before it can be measured.

RAIN GAUGES

Main parts of a rain gauge:

main body

cylinder with collecting funnel fitted into its base

measuring tube

inner canister

inner glass bottle (sometimes placed inside canister)

How the main parts of a rain gauge fit into each other:

cylinder fitted with funnel

inner canister

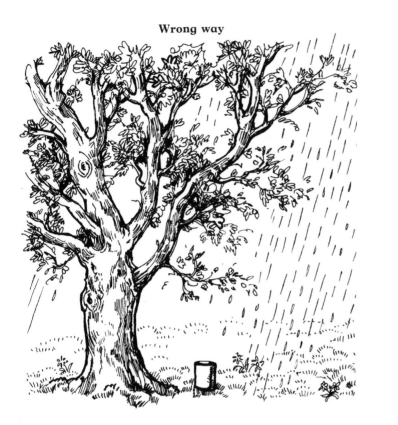

They put a can or bottle with a narrow top
inside the gauge so that the rain cannot get
away easily.

They also have to find a good place for their
rain gauge to make sure that it is not under
trees where water might drip from branches,
or where the leaves could shelter the gauge
from rain.

You can find out how much rain falls where
  you live.
Wait for a day when the clouds look black.
Put a **bucket** outside to catch the rain.
When the rain stops, take a **ruler** and dip it
  into the water at the bottom of the bucket.
You will then be able to say how many
  millimetres of rain fell during the storm.

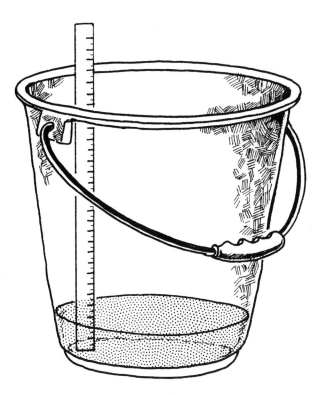

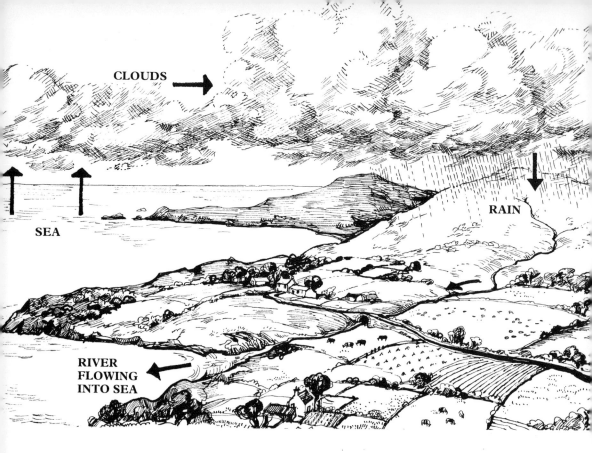

Water from the sea falls on the land as rain,
but always returns to the sea.

If it did not, the oceans would dry up.

The water which evaporates from the sea forms
clouds and these bring rain to the land when
they cool.

Some of this water flows back immediately.

It goes into streams and rivers which carry it
back to the sea.

Some of the water soaks into the soil and, in the end, into rocks underneath the surface of the ground.

It comes to the surface again as **springs.**

These springs bubble as the water comes from under the ground.

The spring water flows into streams and rivers and back to the sea.

The River Usk in Wales

The water in this dam, built across a Swiss valley, is used to make electricity

In many places some **underground** water is used for **tap** water.

Wells are dug into the ground and the water is pumped up into tanks.

Other water comes from **reservoirs.**

Dams have been built across valleys and lakes fill up behind the dams.

Water from the wells and reservoirs is taken by **pipes** to large towns and cities.

But even the water we use at home finds its
    way back to the sea again.
The water with which we flush the lavatory, or
    which empties out of a bath, goes through
    drains to a special place called a **sewage
    works.**
Here, the water is cleaned and piped to a river
    to be returned to the sea.

Some sewers are big enough for sewermen to walk through in order to keep
them clean. This picture shows the Fleet Sewer (once the Fleet River), under
the City of London

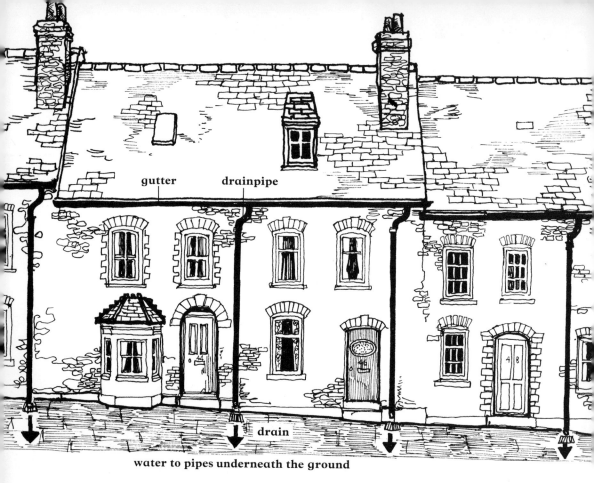

gutter   drainpipe

drain

water to pipes underneath the ground

In an area with main **drainage,** when rain falls
on a house it slides off the roof into the
gutters which lie just under the edge of the
roof (**eaves**).

These gutters take water to a **drainpipe** (or
downpipe), and the water drops into the
drains and pipes below the ground and under
the street.

Water falling on the road or street goes into the
drains at the side of the road.

You have probably seen the drain-hole covers.

When we want water to drain away, we give it
a **slope** to run down.

See how the centre of the road is slightly higher
than the sides (the slope is known as the
camber).

CAMBER

CAMBER

drain

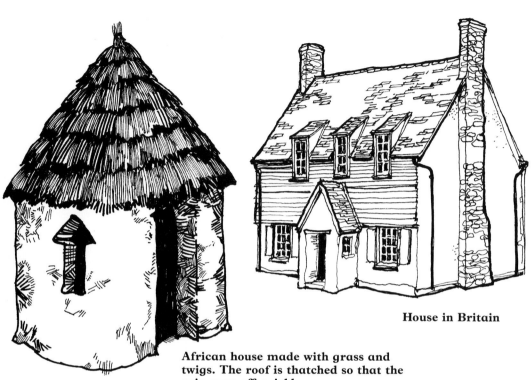

African house made with grass and
twigs. The roof is thatched so that the
rain runs off quickly

House in Britain

In wet lands the houses have to be built in a
   special way.

A flat roof is useless in these places.

Water will form pools and puddles on a **flat**
   roof and may start to leak in.

In these countries, the houses are usually built
   with steeply sloping roofs so that water falls
   quickly away to the gutters.

If the rainfall is always very heavy, the ground
will be wet and may be often flooded.
Then, houses are sometimes built on **stilts** so
that the rooms of the house are dry.

Houses like these
are found in the wet
lands of the Far East,
such as Malaysia and parts of China

Even in temperate countries, like Britain,
houses are usually built so that to get into
them people have to climb up a **step.**
Most houses in Northern Europe have sloping
roofs as well.

Wadi which is nearly dry, but which can become fast-flowing after heavy rain

In very dry lands where rain hardly ever falls, there is no need to build houses with sloping roofs.

Most of the houses in the desert lands of the world have flat roofs.

But even in the desert rain does sometimes fall.

Sudden rainstorms have caused torrents to flow for a few hours in the desert valleys, called **wadis.**

People have camped in these wadis thinking they were dry and safe, only to be drowned in them when a sudden rainstorm bursts.

In the desert where there is no water people have to dig wells to reach underground water

Because heavy rain can do damage when it floods, and because it is needed by farmers, it is useful to know in advance if rain will fall. If floods are expected, everyone can be on the lookout.

Weather forecasts are **broadcast** several times a day, telling us whether rain is likely.

Symbols used by television forecasters to show different kinds of weather. See if you can tell what kind of weather is shown on the map on page 47.

sunny day with no cloud— temperature in °Celsius is given in the centre

sunny intervals

temperature

cloudy—dull weather

cloudy—fine weather

fine-weather clouds and sunny intervals

rain

snow

sleet

showers and sunny intervals

thunderstorms

arrow used to show wind speed and direction

fog
FOG

You can keep an eye on these weather forecasts
    to see if the rain that is forecast does in fact
    fall.
The **forecasters** cannot be certain that rain
    will fall.
But they can say that they *think* it will fall.
Watch the weather forecasts carefully and see
    how often they are right.

INDEX